W9-CPJ-486

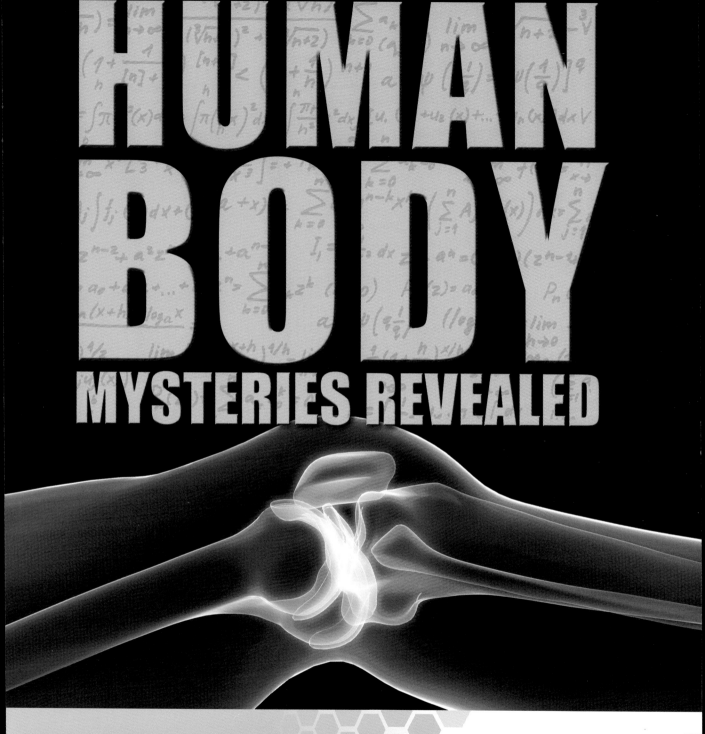

HUMAN BODY
MYSTERIES REVEALED

Natalie Hyde

Author: Natalie Hyde

Editor: Molly Aloian

Proofreader: Crystal Sikkens

Project coordinator: Kathy Middleton

Production coordinator: Katherine Berti

Prepress technician: Katherine Berti

Project editor: Tom Jackson

Designer: Paul Myerscough, Calcium Creative

Picture researcher: Clare Newman

Managing editor: Tim Harris

Art director: Jeni Child

Design manager: David Poole

Editorial director: Lindsey Lowe

Children's publisher: Anne O'Daly

Photographs:
Alamy: Enigma: p. 20 (bottom)
Corbis: Durand Giansantil Perrin/Sygma:
    p. 15 (bottom)
Dreamstime: Frenk And Danielle Kaufmann:
    p. 19
Istockphoto: Sebastian Kaulitzki: p. 7, 9;
    Kenneth Sponsler: p. 29
Science Photo Library: CCI Archives: p. 11 (top); Eye
    of Science: p. 28 (bottom); Hybrid Medical
    Anatomy: p. 26 (bottom);
    Volger Steger: p. 11 (bottom)
Shutterstock: Henk Bentlage: p. 27 (center right);
    Igor Burchenkoc: p. 12–13; Lanev Erickson:
    p. 4–5; Rod Ferris: p. 23; Images Hunter:
    p. 14–15 (bottom); Sebastian Kaulitzki: p. 1; KID:
    p. 8 (top); Axel Kock: p. 20 (top); Rob Marmion:
    p. 17; Mountain Hardcore: p. 16 (top); Kirsty
    Parxgeter: p. 25; Robnroll: p. 21; Sgame: p.
    26–27; Dmitriy Shitonosov: p. 14–15 (top), 28
    (top); James Steidl: p. 10; Suravid: p. 22 (top);
    Jukian Tromeur: p. 30; UK Photo: p. 27 (bottom
    right); Li Wa: p. 16 (bottom); Yakobchuck Vasyl:
    front cover; Ynse: p. 22 (bottom)

Series created by Brown Reference Group

Brown Reference Group have made every attempt to
contact the copyright holders of all pictures used in this
work. Please contact info@brownreference.com if you
have any information identifying copyright ownership.

Library and Archives Canada Cataloguing in Publication

Hyde, Natalie, 1963-
    Human body mysteries revealed / Natalie Hyde.

(Mysteries revealed)
Includes index.
ISBN 978-0-7787-7415-0 (bound).--ISBN 978-0-7787-7430-3 (pbk.)

    1. Human physiology--Juvenile literature. I. Title.
II. Series: Mysteries revealed (St. Catharines, Ont.)

QP37.H93 2010   j612   C2009-906262-3

Library of Congress Cataloging-in-Publication Data

Hyde, Natalie, 1963-
 Human body mysteries revealed / Natalie Hyde.
    p. cm. -- (Mysteries revealed)
Includes index.
 ISBN 978-0-7787-7415-0 (reinforced lib. bd.g : alk. paper)
-- ISBN 978-0-7787-7430-3 (pbk. : alk. paper)
1. Human physiology--Juvenile literature. I. Title. II. Series.

 QP37.H995 2010
 612--dc22
                                                    2009042770

Crabtree Publishing Company

Printed in the U.S.A./122009/BG20091103

Published in Canada
Crabtree Publishing
616 Welland Ave.
St. Catharines, Ontario
L2M 5V6

Published in the United States
Crabtree Publishing
PMB 59051
350 Fifth Avenue, 59th Floor
New York, New York 10118

Contents

Introduction

The human body begins as just a single cell. The cell divides in two, and keeps splitting over and over— until there are a trillion cells working together. With so much going on inside, we are still figuring out how the human body works.

The human body has its own electricity, plumbing system, central heating, and power plants. With incredibly strong but flexible parts it can lock, bend, and stretch so we can perform **intricate** movements such as a twisting dance move, skateboard trick, or a full court shot in basketball. The human body not only works day after day, but it is also ready in case something goes wrong. Its defense system fights off invaders and mends body parts when injury strikes.

Looking inside

Even though we have been studying the human body for centuries, we are still learning new things. With powerful microscopes we can look deeper into cells and see how they power our muscles. Computer-powered scanners allow us to watch our brains thinking—and even dreaming. Almost every day, we unlock another mystery about the wonders of the human body.

cell The smallest body part of all, cells are the building blocks of a living body

The human body can do many things. It can run, jump, and swim, but also mend itself and even think!

intricate Very complex, with many small details

How much of our brain do we use?

You might have heard that people use only one-tenth of their brains—and only a genius makes use of the whole thing. This is not true.

Our brains are complex machines that do thousands of jobs all at once. We do not use all of our brain at the same time. Different parts turn on when there is a certain job to be done.

Thinking space

The lower part of the brain looks after body processes, such as balance and feeling hunger. The front section, or **forebrain**, is where we do our thinking. The left side of the forebrain understands language and uses logic to figure out math and other puzzles. The right side is where our imagination creates new ideas.

"**If the brain were so simple we could understand it, we would be so simple we couldn't.**"
Lyall Watson

Large blood vessels supply the brain with fuel called **glucose**.

forebrain The largest part of the brain which fills the top of your skull

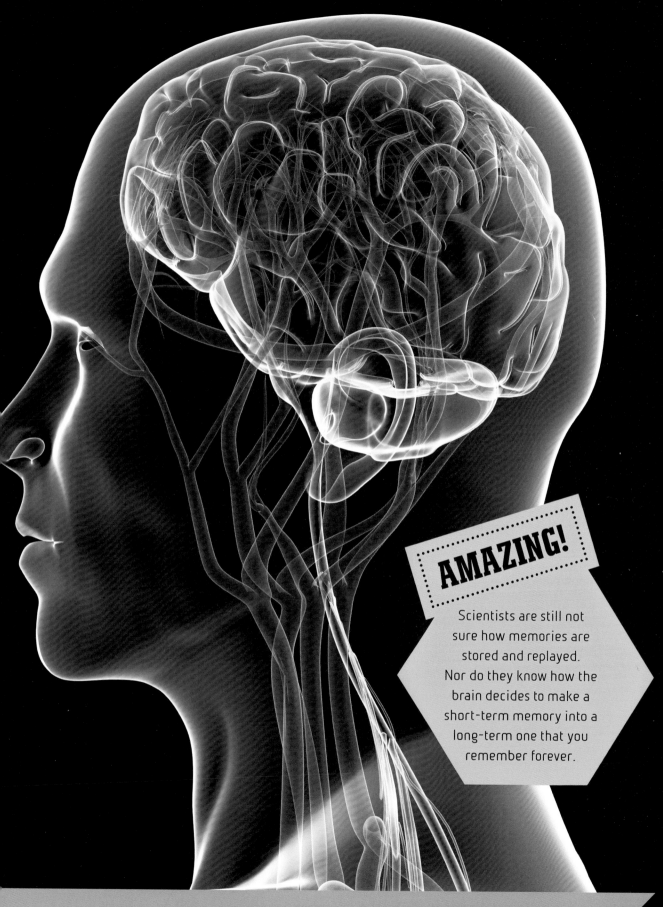

AMAZING!

Scientists are still not sure how memories are stored and replayed. Nor do they know how the brain decides to make a short-term memory into a long-term one that you remember forever.

glucose A simple type of sugar which is the only thing that can power the brain

What is the brain made of?

Three-quarters of the brain is water and most of the rest is fat. That makes the brain look like a wobbly gray blob. But inside is the most complicated system in the Universe! The brain has billions of cells called **neurons**. Neurons work like wires and can send and receive electric signals. Neurons are connected into a network that carries messages around the brain. Each neuron is linked to dozens of its neighbors. When you learn something, new connections are made so that you can remember it.

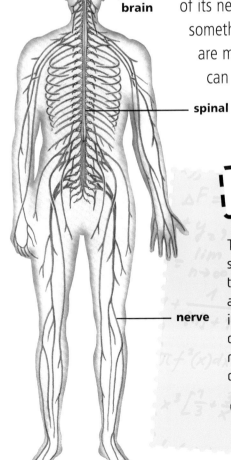

brain

spinal cord

nerve

⬤ Neurons are coated in fat which keeps the electricity in—like the plastic cover around copper wires.

SCIENCE EXPLAINED

The brain is the command center for the body's nervous system. Information comes into the brain from the rest of the body along the **spinal cord**—and orders go back out again the same way. The spinal cord is very important and is protected inside the bones of your spine. If the spinal cord is broken, your brain cannot talk to the body, and you may become paralyzed. Nerves branch off the spine, carrying messages to and from all parts of the body.

◀ Electric pulses move along nerves at 62 miles per hour (90 km/h).

neurons Nerve cells; they have a central body with dozens of branches

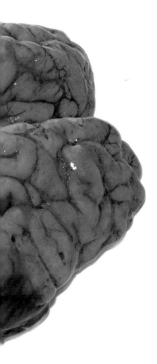

How is electricity used for thinking?

Pulses of electricity travel from one neuron to another in the brain, turning the cells on and off like switches in a computer. A pulse is produced by chemicals flooding through the walls of the neuron, which makes a wave of electricity flow along the wirelike cells.

⬢ Making the electricity in our brain's neurons takes up one-fifth of all our energy.

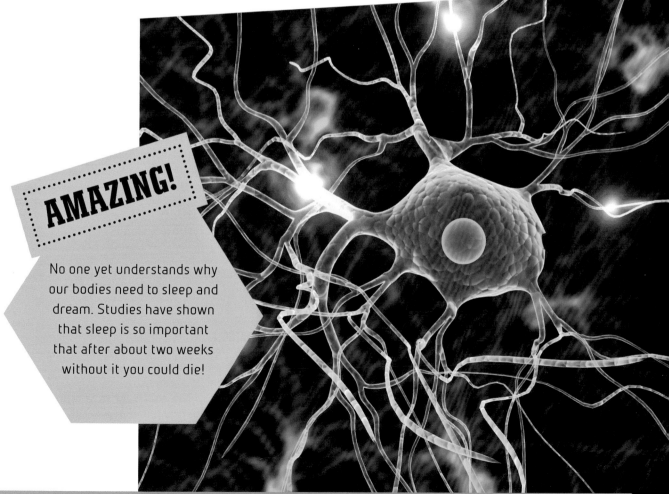

AMAZING!

No one yet understands why our bodies need to sleep and dream. Studies have shown that sleep is so important that after about two weeks without it you could die!

Can we see inside a living brain?

Yes! The brain is very soft so it does not show up in X-rays like bones do. Instead, doctors use an MRI scanner to take pictures of the brain. MRI stands for "magnetic resonance imaging." The scanner contains a huge magnet which turns your body into a kind of magnet, too. Then the scanner fires radio waves through you, which bend due to the effects of the magnet. A computer reads the radio echoes to make a picture of your insides. MRI scans are used to look for cancers and bleeding inside the brain. Other scanners use **radioactive** chemicals to watch how different parts of the brain are working together.

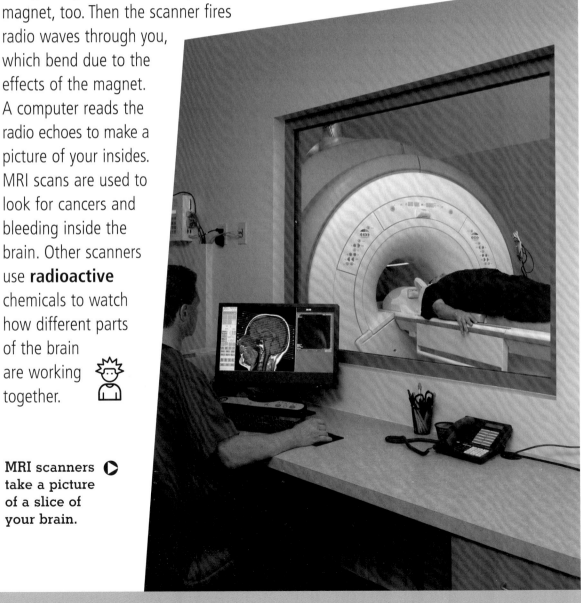

MRI scanners ◗ take a picture of a slice of your brain.

radioactive Giving off high-energy beams of radiation

HISTORY EXPLAINED

Trepanning was an early type of brain surgery. A drill or spike was used to make a hole in a person's skull. The hole was meant to release demons from the head. People believed that evil spirits caused headaches and mental problems. Scientists have found skulls with drill holes in from thousands of years ago. Some of the skulls show healing marks around the hole, proving that the patients survived the operation.

◀ Instructions on trepanning in a medical book from the 1300s.

Could you transplant a brain?

This headset picks up brain activity, so the man can control an **avatar** just by thinking. ◉

Doctors could move a brain into a new skull, but it could not communicate with its new body—the spinal cord cannot be reconnected. Just moving the part of the brain that stores memories might work better, if we knew which bit to move. In the future, people might be able to save ideas and memories on a computer, and download them into another brain.

---

avatar A movable image that represents a player in a virtual game

Why can't we live forever?

The body is good at mending itself. But, it cannot fix things so they are as good as new. There are always a few mistakes. As you get older, your body collects these weaknesses until, eventually, it stops working.

Scientists have discovered that parts of the body die all the time. Cells are set to die before they get too damaged to work properly. The **DNA** in a cell has chemical tags on the end. One tag is lost each time a cell divides, and once they are all gone the cell cannot divide again— and it dies. The body needs new cells to mend injuries and defend itself. An old body has run out of most of its dividing cells, and so takes a long time to heal. Eventually a problem will kill the body before it can fix itself.

> **"I intend to live forever, or die trying."**
> **Groucho Marx**

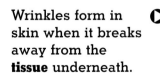

Wrinkles form in skin when it breaks away from the **tissue** underneath.

DNA The chemical that carries the instructions for how our body grows and works

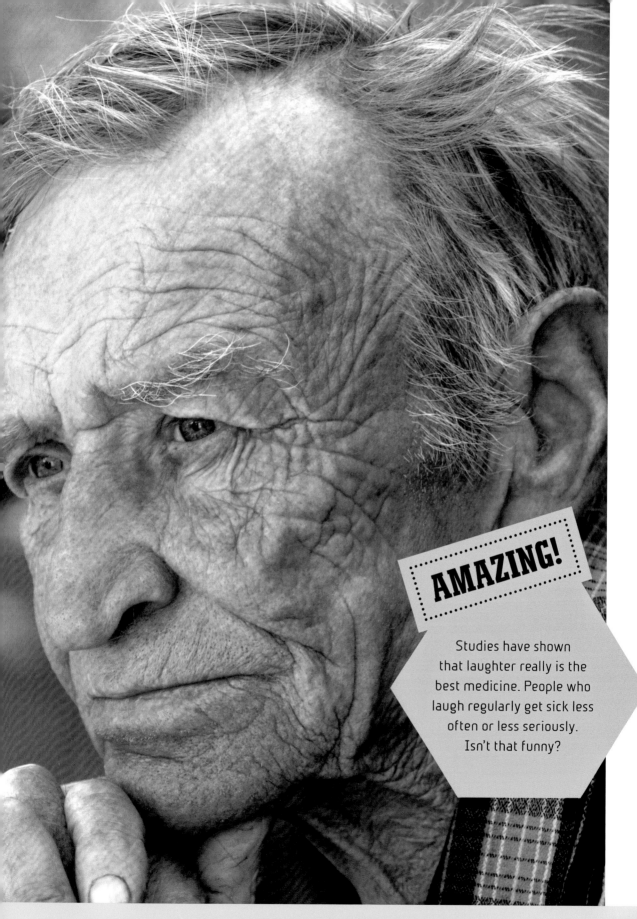

AMAZING!

Studies have shown that laughter really is the best medicine. People who laugh regularly get sick less often or less seriously. Isn't that funny?

tissue A group of body cells that work together to do a certain job

How do bones mend themselves?

Bones are not hard, dead supports like the girders in a house. They are just as alive as the rest of your body. When a bone breaks, the body starts working immediately to fix it. Cells near the break begin to make **cartilage** to connect the two pieces. Cartilage is not as strong as bone, so once the gap is filled in, the body begins to replace the cartilage with bone cells. Blood is diverted to the break to make sure there is enough energy to make new bone. Once the bone is re-formed, calcium and phosphorous are added to make it strong again. While the body can do all this by itself, a doctor must make sure that the bone is lined up properly.

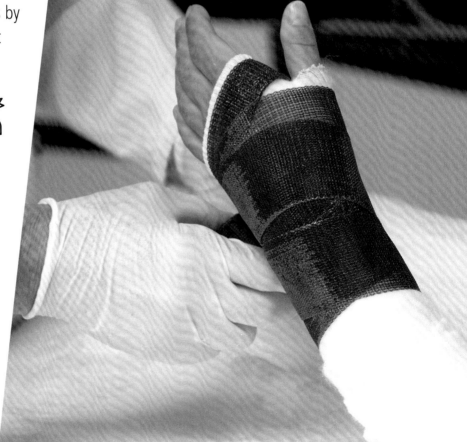

A hard plaster cast keeps the bones still so the arm mends straight.

cartilage A bendy tissue that connects bones at joints and is in the ears and nose

Why does exercise make me fitter?

When you exercise, the fibers in your muscles get torn slightly. When the body repairs the tears, it makes each of the fibers a little thicker. (During the repair you feel stiff and might ache a little.) The thicker muscles are stronger so next time you can run faster and farther.

◀ Keeping active makes all your muscles strong.

HISTORY EXPLAINED

Some drugs called steroids help the cells make more **proteins** and build up muscle tissue faster. A few athletes decided to taking steroids as they trained. The drugs helped them recover faster and get stronger more easily. The drugs made them winners. But other athletes and sports officials felt using drugs like this was a dangerous way to cheat. Using steroids can badly damage the heart and liver, and so they are banned from sports.

In 1988, the sprinter Ben Johnson lost his ▶ Olympic gold medal for using steroids.

proteins The chemicals used to build muscles, skin, and most other body parts

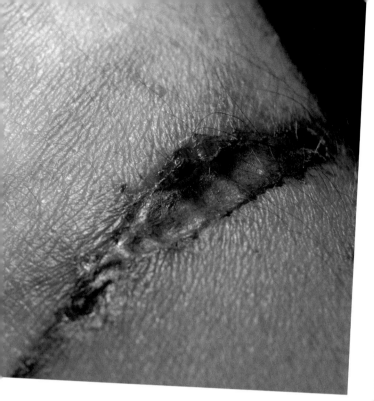

How does blood close up cuts?

If the skin is damaged, blood from broken vessels flows into the hole. The blood's job is to fill the cut, and it does this by turning solid, or clotting. Blood clots are formed by small cells called platelets in the blood. They clump together and a mesh of the protein fibrin gathers around them. The fibrin mesh forms a scab over the wound as the skin heals beneath.

A scab is a temporary cover to stop any germs from getting into the skin.

SCIENCE EXPLAINED

Blood carries **oxygen** to where it is needed in the body. However, blood cells come in four types. Do you know your blood type? The blood groups are called, A, B, AB, and O. Blood produces markers, or antigens, according to its blood type. AB blood produces both A and B markers, while O blood has no antigens at all. Blood also contains **antibodies**, which attack blood from other types. AB blood does not attack any blood types—it accepts all types of antigens, but O blood will attack all blood except the O type.

People need extra blood during surgery, and it must match their blood type.

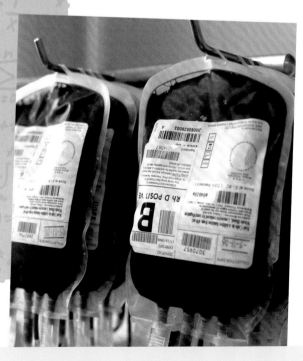

oxygen The gas from the air that is used by the body to burn fuel for energy

Why do I get hot when I'm sick?

White blood cells are the body's security guards. As soon as they detect intruders, such as viruses, in the system, they send signals to the hypothalamus, a region at the bottom of the brain. The hypothalamus controls how warm the body is, and begins to make it hotter to help fight off the invasion. A high temperature helps the body in two ways. Many invaders are killed by the heat. The body's processes also speed up so it can produce more white blood cells to fight the germs.

◗ Sick people should check their temperature. If it gets very high their brain can stop working properly.

AMAZING!

People who fall into icy water have been known to survive under the water. The cold makes the heart slow down and only pump blood to the brain. The cold water refrigerates the rest of the body and keeps it from dying.

When is it time to wake up?

Your body has a clock. Scientists call it the circadian rhythm. It is a roughly 24-hour cycle of body processes. All living things use this same rhythm.

Body clocks are not very accurate. The word circadian means "about a day," and the clock needs to be reset regularly. The body picks up the pattern of light and dark to set the clock. The rhythm makes you feel tired at night, and wake up in the morning—not the other way around. The clock also controls the body's temperature, the production of **hormones**, and even brain activity. People suffering from jet lag have flown to a place where night and day happens at different times to their circadian rhythm. They feel tired in the day, but can't sleep at night.

If you are getting enough sleep, you should wake up at the same time each morning.

hormones Chemical messengers that control many body functions

AMAZING!

Sleepwalking is a **disorder** where a person acts like they are awake but is in fact still asleep. Sleepwalkers usually have their eyes open but are slow to answer questions. Once awake again, they can't remember a thing.

disorder When the body or mind is not working properly

What keeps us breathing when we are asleep?

We need to breathe all the time, so breathing happens without us having to think about it. Breathing is controlled by the brain stem. We breathe in air to collect more oxygen, and breathe out air to get rid of **carbon dioxide**. When carbon dioxide builds up in the blood, our brain orders the body to breath faster to get rid of it. We make more carbon dioxide when we are running fast, so we start breathing faster to get rid of it

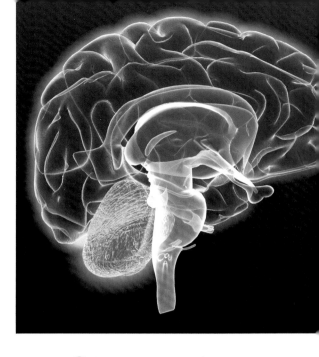

⬤ The brain stem (shown in yellow) controls automatic functions such as heart beat and digestion as well as breathing.

◀ Air is invisible but on cold days the **water vapor** in your breath turns to a cloud of steam

carbon dioxide A gas made by the body when we burn our food fuel

Why do we have two ears but just one nose?

It might not look like it but you have two noses—at least two halves. Each nostril connects to a hollow area in each cheek, known as the nasal cavity. The lining of the cavity picks up chemicals in the air passing through the nose. You sense these chemicals as odors. If one side of your nose stops working, you can smell fine with the other. The big difference between the ears and nose is that nostrils are side by side and the ears are far apart. Odors arrive at each nostril at the same time. However, a noise reaches one ear slightly before it hits the other. The brain uses the time difference to figure out the direction of the sound.

Ears pick up waves traveling through the air—from all directions.

How does the stomach not digest itself?

The liquid in the stomach is a strong **acid** that fizzes away at the food. Stomach enzymes also break up the food into simpler substances, such as sugar and fat, that can be absorbed through the stomach lining. The stomach is lined with **mucus** that is alkaline—the opposite of acid. The mucus lets food through, but blocks the enzymes and reacts with the acid. People with thin mucus layers get dangerous sores on the lining called stomach ulcers.

◖ Digestion begins in the mouth, where the food is chewed into a mush and mixed with enzymes in the saliva.

SCIENCE EXPLAINED

Enzymes are the body's tool kit. They are not just used for digestion. Everything that happens in a cell—making DNA or energy—is controlled by an enzyme. Enzymes are protein molecules, with complicated folded shapes (right). The shape is very important. Digestive enzymes first fit around sugars or fats and then break them apart. Other enzymes join chemicals together.

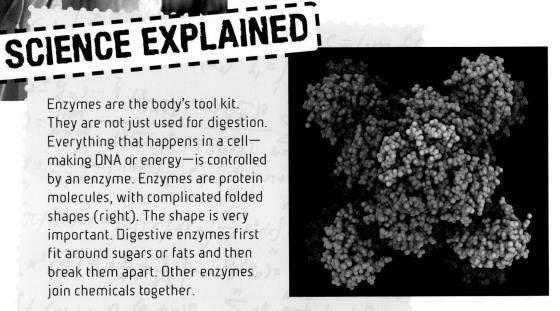

acid A chemical that attacks other substances, breaking them apart

Why do muscles get tired?

Muscles need a supply of oxygen to power themselves. The oxygen is delivered by the blood and used to burn sugar and release energy. The waste product is carbon dioxide, which is taken away by the blood. However, when the muscles are working hard, the blood cannot get enough oxygen to them fast enough, so they begin to burn sugar without oxygen. The waste product now is a substance called lactic acid, which builds up in the muscles. The acid attacks the muscle fibers, producing a burning sensation, which we call muscle ache.

⚪ Breathing deeply will help to stop your muscles from getting tired when they are working hard.

AMAZING!

Michel Lotito is better known as Monsieur Mangetout (Mr. Eat Everything). The French entertainer would eat almost anything—he even cut up a small airplane and swallowed it!

What is the code of life?

Inside almost every cell in your body is a secret code that contains instructions for making a new you.

The code is stored on DNA, or deoxyribonucleic acid. DNA is a chain of chemicals that is shaped like a twisted ladder, or helix. The rungs of this ladder are made up of pairs of chemicals called bases. There are four different bases, adenine, guanine, cytosine, and thymine, or A, G, C, and T. Reading down the side of a DNA strand, each set of three bases creates codes for an **amino acid**. Each amino acid is one ingredient in the recipe for a certain protein. Proteins are the building blocks of everything in your body, from enzymes to muscles.

"We've discovered the secret of life."
Francis Crick (one of the discoverers of DNA)

Your DNA has 6 billion base pairs but is easily small enough to fit on the period at the end of this sentence.

amino acid A type of chemical that is chained together to make proteins

AMAZING!

You might think that
humans have the most DNA—
after all we are pretty complicated
animals. Actually that honor goes
to a tiny **single-celled** creature
called the *Amoeba dubia*,
which has 200 times more
DNA than humans.

single-celled When a life form has a body containing just one cell

Where is DNA stored?

A cell's DNA is not one long continuous strand. It is divided into coiled sections called chromosomes. Each chromosome contains many groups of base pairs that carry the code for one protein or control one part of how your body functions or looks. The groups are called **genes** and may affect the way your skin looks, how good you are at catching balls, or the sound of your voice.

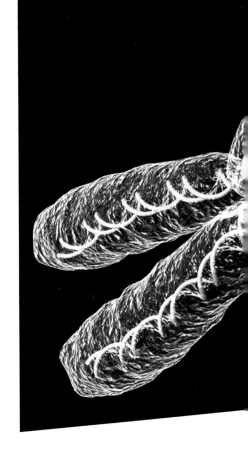

A human cell has 46 chromosomes—23 come ▶ from the father and 23 from the mother.

What happens if genes go wrong?

Before a cell divides the DNA makes a copy of itself, called replication. Sometimes mistakes are made, and the copied genes have faulty instructions. Cancer is caused by problems with genes that control how a cell divides. The cells keep on dividing and cannot be stopped. They grow into a lump, or **tumor**, which damages healthy body parts.

◀ Doctors hope to find cancers early, before the faulty cells spread through the body.

genes A piece of DNA that is passed on from parents to their children

SCIENCE EXPLAINED

Mistakes, or accidental changes, in DNA code are called mutations. Most mutations have no effect on the body because they are in parts of the gene that do not carry instructions. Nearly all other mutations end up killing the body—or keep it from growing in the first place. However, a tiny number of mutations actually make a body work better. These helpful mutations are what makes evolution possible. The mutations create a slightly different type of life form, which might be better at staying alive than the older versions. And so the life form slowly changes, or evolves.

Scientists think polar bears are grizzly bears with a mutant gene for white hair.

Can we change our genes?

Scientists have found several genes that cause diseases. But what do they do next? In future gene therapy they might be able to replace faulty genes with ones that work properly. One technique being studied is using a virus to "infect" the patient with the new genes.

⬭ We get genes from our parents, and sometimes dangerous genes are passed on.

SCIENCE EXPLAINED

For centuries, people have been changing the way animals look and what they do by breeding them. This process takes years and can only make small changes. Today **genetic** engineers can take a gene from one plant or animal and put it into another **species**. Genetically modified (GM) organisms have genes added from completely unrelated species. For example, frost-resistant tomatoes have genes from a fish that lives in cold water. The gene helps the tomato grow in cold weather. Some countries have banned GM plants because there are concerns about them spreading into the wild.

⬭ This mouse was given a gene to make a protein that glows in the dark.

genetic To do with the study of genes

Will clones take over the world?

○ Identical twins are natural clones—they share the same genes.

Clones do not have a father or mother—they are a copy of another animal and have the same set of genes. A complete set of DNA is taken from a cell and injected into an egg. The egg is treated with chemicals and an electric current so it begins dividing. The egg is then placed in the womb and left to grow just like a normal baby. Scientists have cloned sheep, pigs, mice, rabbits, and cows, but no humans have been cloned. Artificial clones have many problems and often die young from diseases.

AMAZING!

The DNA sections between the genes on the chromosomes were once named "junk DNA" because scientists did not believe it had any purpose. Now new studies are finding clues that there may be hidden instructions in all that code.

Human Body Facts

The surface area of your lungs is the same as a tennis court.

Your heart beats about 100,000 times a day.

Our skin is our largest organ, about 22 square feet (2 sq. m).

The body has 639 muscles.

Find Out More

Books

The Way We Work: Getting to Know the Amazing Human Body by David Macaulay, Houghton Mifflin Books for Children, 2008.

Dr Frankenstein's Human Body Book by Richard Walker, Dorling Kindersley, 2008.

Let's Relate to Genetics, Crabtree Publishing, 2009.

Web sites

How Stuff Works: The Immune System
health.howstuffworks.com/immune-system8.htm

Body Basics Library
kidshealth.org/teen/your_body/
    body_basics/body_basics.html

National Geographic: Human Body
science.nationalgeographic.com/science/
    health-and-human-body/human-body

Glossary

acid A chemical that attacks other substances, breaking them apart

amino acid A type of chemical that is chained together to make proteins

antibodies Chemicals in the body that search for invaders and attack them

avatar A movable image that represents a player in a virtual game

carbon dioxide A gas made by the body when we burn our food fuel

cartilage A bendy tissue that connects bones at joints and is in the ears and nose

cell The smallest body part of all, cells are the building blocks of a living body

disorder When the body or mind is not working properly

DNA The chemical that carries the instructions for how our body grows and works

forebrain The largest part of the brain which fills the top of your skull

genes A piece of DNA that is passed on from parents to their children

genetic To do with the study of genes

glucose A simple type of sugar which is the only thing that can power the brain

hormones Chemical messengers that control many body functions

intricate Very complex, with many small details

mucus The slimy stuff made by your body—especially in the nose

neurons Nerve cells; they have a central body with dozens of branches

oxygen The gas from the air that is used by the body to burn fuel for energy

proteins The chemicals used to build muscles, skin, and most other body parts

radioactive Giving off high-energy beams of radiation

single-celled When a life form has a body containing just one cell

species A type of animal or plant that is different from any other

spinal cord A bundle of nerves in the back that controls simple body movements

tissue A group of body cells that work together to do a certain job

tumor A group of cells that grow inside the body where they are not needed

water vapor The gas form of water

Index